PRAISE FOR JACQUELINE PIRTLE

"Jacqueline takes you always directly to what you are ready to see or experience."

— LONGTIME CLIENT AND READER

"It is liberating to face your own blocks and to be finally free of the weight that they have caused for many years. And while for me the changes I'm experiencing are noticeable and real, I still feel like myself. Just a more sure self."

— LONGTIME CLIENT AND READER

"Jacqueline makes me BELIEVE I can be and live a joyful and magical existence every new day of my life!"

— LONGTIME CLIENT AND READER

JACQUELINE PIRTLE

MAGICK AND BROOMSTICKS

THE PORTAL
TO YOUR WILD SIDE

A 30 day journal

COPYRIGHT

Copyright © 2021 Jacqueline Pirtle
www.FreakyHealer.com

All rights reserved. No part of this book may be reproduced or transmitted in any form or by any means, electronic or mechanical, including photocopying, recording, or by any information storage and retrieval system without the written permission of the publisher, except where permitted by law.

ISBN-13: 978-1-955059-31-2

Publisher: Freaky Healer

Editor-in-chief: Zoe Pirtle
All-round Support: Mitch Pirtle

Book cover design by Kingwood Creations kingwoodcreations.com

Author photo courtesy of Lionel Madiou madious.com

I want to let you know that all my books and work as a holistic practitioner are a wholesome system, supporting you to live a more conscious, mindful, and happier life.

However, I made it so you can receive the benefit of living more joyously solely by working through this terrific journal book, while also experiencing the full satisfaction in continuing on to the next journal of this series—not to mention the rock solid tools you get by reading any of my other books or adding in my podcast *The Daily Freak*. Either way, I know you'll love my inspirational teachings.

Find out more at:
FreakyHealer.com
Amazon - Jacqueline Pirtle's Author Page
The Daily Freak Podcast

Before you dive in, I want to thank you for hopping on the magick train with me! I truly hope you enjoy **Magick and Broomsticks** as much as I loved writing it, and if you do, it would be wonderful if you could take a short minute and leave a review on Amazon and Goodreads.com as soon as you can.

Your kind feedback helps other readers find my books more easily, and to be happy faster. Consider it a joy-deed for the world.

Thank you!

ACKNOWLEDGMENTS

Let's be honest here… I have a dream team!

I could not have finished this book without the help of talented, creative, high-for-life, and phenomenal professionals.

From the bottom of my heart, I want to thank Zoe Pirtle for her editorial mastery; Mitch Pirtle for his all-round support; kingwoodcreations.com for their fun and polished book cover design; and madiouART.com for an amazing photo shoot.

I'd also like to extend a huge "Thank You!" to all fans of my work and books—I created this beautiful journal series for you.

Life is spectacular with you on my side!

"You came for magick, and that is what I will give you!"
Your life says with its charming ways.

DEDICATION

I dedicate this journal to all magick seekers and challenge them to jet off on their broomsticks without hesitation, only eagerness.

INTRODUCTION

Hello wild one,

This journal-book could not come at a more magickal time because the belief that the enchantment in the world is not present anymore has snuck itself into the existence of many. That is understandable in these very intense times, but then again, is it really—since we are the sole-creator of how we experience life and own the whole business of what we make out of it?

Here is a great example of what I mean with this:

The other day I was biking at the waterfront and saw a dark kind of hump in the water. My initial thought was that it's a dolphin - I love dolphins - so I slowed down to enjoy that moment and to see that magick again. But nothing and more nothing showed itself. I mumbled, "Come on, show yourself again—you got about 5 seconds to verify that you really are a dolphin and not a bird." I love birds too, but dolphins lift my spirit even higher. Still, there was nothing.

Right then it occurred to me how much I needed to see that dolphin in order to believe in its magickal presence—even though I had seen dolphins at that spot before and knew they are, indeed, there.

INTRODUCTION

Think about that, needing visible verification to see the magick before actively believing in it!

It's so easy to live in that un-magickal mode since we practiced it so many times and to this day still do exactly that. So, I had three options in that scenario:

- Claim my life-creator job by moving along and believing it to be a dolphin - seeing or not seeing it - since that is what I wanted it to be and enjoy the magick I am creating for myself.
- Give away my life-creator job, and keep watching until it shows itself again while waiting for magick to happen with the possible outcome of running out of time or a grand disappointment.
- Move along, leave it as unidentified—missing out on possible magick, being a passenger in my own life.

I chose to have my dolphin!

Every split second in life has these three options, and you get to choose the most magickal one every single time. So what are you waiting for?

You are a whole being comprised of a physical body, mind, soul, and consciousness, here to experience life through physicality and your soul being—magicking into *bigger* and *more* at all times through human-ness and from the core of the energetic essence that makes everything and everyone.

As part of that energetic bundle you are vibrating in frequencies, some lower than others but preferably higher ones, since that's where the magick is. The best thing is that you are capable of making your own magick, no matter what physicality or others are showing up as, by focusing on what YOU want it to be —whether that is a dolphin, a bird, or nothing.

Living a magickal existence skyrockets you into your own wild magick, and there a powerful broomstick awaits; one that

INTRODUCTION

jets you higher and higher into living more heroic than you have ever been and with the grandest wisdom you have ever had. Breathing as such means you are experiencing though your energetic part - your soul being, your inner you, your higher self, however you wish to call it - but also from your one-ness with consciousness, where all the fun is held.

This **Magick and Broomsticks** journal exists to help you live through your wild side and create the magick that you want by tickling your imaginary ways, turning your gunkiness upside down and inside out—from there, you can find new and fresh magick that fits the charm you want in life.

I say, let your flying broom get you to that magick-land with speed, so you can create a life where an ocean of opportunities will catch hold of you and the excitement of living a life filled with incredible manifestations is never in question.

Journaling through this 30 day edition of **Magick and Broomsticks** gives your most magickal version of you the spotlight and brings a huge heightening into the equation so you can experience life like you never have before, craft a time beyond your dreams, and love what you live—to become a master in living consciously, mindfully, and feeling phenomenal while manifesting the best of the best. It's a change that is forever!

As a side note, there are a couple of bonus days at the end in case you ever find the need to do two entries in a day, or so you can keep writing while you wait for the next journal in this series to arrive. I also left you a few blank *Magick and Broomsticks* pages to journal about deepening your ways of being magickaly alive.

Enough chit-chat, I know you are ready—so grab your pen and have incredible fun catching more magick than you have ever caught in your new enchanted ways.

Happiest,
    Jacqueline

 Day 1

IMAGINE life is offering you a huge treasure trunk. Make it the most spectacular chest that you have ever seen, with everything included for you to become the master magick-magician of all time—so powerful that all that's needed to take matters into your own hands to create whatever magick you wish for in life, you already have it.

With the utmost excitement you open that super-power box and start unpacking, while being in wonder and awe!

Here's what is in there for sure:

A spellbinding book a.k.a. this journal, a bewitching hat, and an entrancing broomstick for you to speed into infinity together with your magick.

But what else will your chest include, and what personal items are there to unpack?

_____
_____
_____
_____
_____
_____
_____
_____
_____
_____
_____
_____

Magick and Broomsticks - The Portal to Your Wild Side

# Day 2

Now that you're all decked out for the most impressive magick-creation action and for sure ready to be on your wild side, what is the *impossible* that you are wishing for yourself to be possible? What craziness that seems unreal to you are you looking to make your new normal?

Make this list endless and keep coming back to scratch what has been revealed as done—but also add on new and fresh endeavors that you are inspired to pursue.

_____
_____
_____
_____
_____
_____
_____
_____
_____
_____
_____
_____
_____
_____
_____
_____
_____
_____
_____

Magick and Broomsticks - The Portal to Your Wild Side

 ay 3

TAKE YOUR LIST OF IMPOSSIBLE. Pick one or many of these items, and focus your magick on them—to make them possible in your own magick-creator world.

Is one to be happier? Imagine dancing through your new day.

Is another to be healthier? Visualize your physical body being a wonderland of wellness, there to be enjoyed at all times.

Could your wish be for more money? Pretend to climb a money mountain, just to slide down on the other side with happy shrieks.

Or are you wishing for a new job? How about imagining to be a king or queen for the day?

You get the gist—make your impossible possible in your magick world, and then see what happens!

___

Magick and Broomsticks - The Portal to Your Wild Side

 ay 4

LET'S work - if you can even call it working, ha! - on your unreal crazy lineup on your list. The *unreal* is only a word on paper, aside from being an energy that you can cleanse—since everything is always possible and you can create your own experience in life at any time.

So, how can you make things more real for you?

The answer is, through imagination, visualization, thoughts and feelings, and also believing into the realness of these things.

Plus, why does it even seem crazy if you want it so much, and since what you want is your truth? Go on, no more tricking yourself out of things!

Magick and Broomsticks - The Portal to Your Wild Side

 ay 5

YOUR BROOMSTICK IS ready for takeoff! Where will you go—and is it upward, downward, or straight ahead? Why are you going there—what are your expectations? Do you have a plan, or would you rather take the spontaneous route? How far will you fly—and is there even a limit? Fly, magick one, fly!

Magick and Broomsticks - The Portal to Your Wild Side

 ay 6

PICK a cloud and have your own heightening experience—puffy, dreamy, fluffy, and atop the world. Go on, use your best imagination for this! Be choosy of your fitting cloud, then hop on up, or even better, slip on in. How does it feel, sitting or jumping on top? How is it to be engulfed in it—quiet, peaceful, like in a beautiful nothing-ness? Oh, how well you are doing your job as the magician that you naturally are.

Magick and Broomsticks - The Portal to Your Wild Side

 ay 7

IMAGINE CLIMBING in a tree - or actually go climb - and pretend to be a little insect, a bird, or a squirrel living and playing in that green paradise like it's your own magick-wonderland! How does that feel for you?

Next, imagine you are the bark, the roots, the leaves, and the fruit or flower of that tree—how does this feel?

Visualize breathing in and enjoying the sun, rain, wind, and all storms as that tree. What does this magick spark?

Are you inspired and regenerated yet?

_____
_____
_____
_____
_____
_____
_____
_____
_____
_____
_____
_____
_____
_____
_____
_____

Magick and Broomsticks - The Portal to Your Wild Side

# Day 8

HAVE you ever hopped on a rainbow? It's about time! Close your eyes and take the jump.

How does it feel to live on those colors, but also through the brilliance of their glimmer? Do you like the fun fact the bend of that rainbow brings - like a bridge - and where could that bend lead to? How about the height this rainbow sits, do you like the bird's eye view of things? And lastly, all the people looking upward to your rainbow in awe and happiness; does that make you feel like you are indeed living a magickal experience?

_____
_____
_____
_____
_____
_____
_____
_____
_____
_____
_____
_____
_____
_____
_____
_____
_____

Magick and Broomsticks - The Portal to Your Wild Side

 Day 9

A BROOMSTICK CAN BE USED in many ways—to fly, to defend, to show off, or to set the tone to where you want it to be—with only the last mentioned fact needing an explanation.

Imagine you standing with a broomstick. Now, visualize yourself standing without one—with it you look even more powerful, mystical, and somewhat unpredictable to many, which is an added energy to your wholesome you meaning you will radiate this added essence to your surroundings because your energetic value changed.

So, will you please walk your journey with your magick-mop energy attached to you—or even better, will you take the magick flight?

___

Magick and Broomsticks - The Portal to Your Wild Side

 ay 10

PICK your perfectly adventurous mountain to climb! Make it as tall and big - or as flat and small - as you like and then, after a swift hike, imagine standing at the tippy top. Breathe and spread your arms like you mean it. Remember, it's your mountain and you own this place! How does that feel? Powerful, strong, vital, like you are on top of THE mountain? Go on, magick warrior, live your new day as such!

_____
_____
_____
_____
_____
_____
_____
_____
_____
_____
_____
_____
_____
_____
_____
_____
_____
_____
_____
_____

Magick and Broomsticks - The Portal to Your Wild Side

 Day 11

DEVOURING your favorite cupcake is magick—one that is real, logical, and believable since you taste it and others can see you enjoying it.

What other easily believable magick is there for you right now? How can you consciously become one with that awesomeness?

___

Magick and Broomsticks - The Portal to Your Wild Side

 ay 12

Yesterday we covered all logical enchantments. Today, we dig into the otherworldly ones that are at many times hard to believe in—like the non-physically sensing ones.

Are there any magickal happenings that you can't explain—like your inner being, the support that life offers, the love in the air? How will you experience that magick more often?

Magick and Broomsticks - The Portal to Your Wild Side

 ay 13

WHAT FLOWER ARE you going to land on today—how does it look, smell, and feel? Close your eyes and make your grand landing, then magickaly expand on it like you have no limits. Play on it like it's the biggest playground you have ever been on, and dance on it like a wild one since that is the normal behavior of a resident living in this flower land. How does that feel, what magick are you creating here, and how much silliness is sprouting for you?

___

Magick and Broomsticks - The Portal to Your Wild Side

 Day 14

You can have all the magick in this physical world—you deserve it since it's your birthright!

What will it be?

Let this spark inspiration for yourself and for others, for your private life, your work existence, and also for your home and public surroundings.

Magick and Broomsticks - The Portal to Your Wild Side

 ay 15

LET'S pump your worthiness even higher: You can have all the magick in the energetic realm too—you know, all the unseeable, untouchable, and unexplainable!

That's exciting! So what emotional, mind-blowing, and soul aligning magick will it be?

Remember, limitless is an energetic truth—go all out here!

___

Magick and Broomsticks - The Portal to Your Wild Side

Day 16

WHERE ARE YOU RIGHT NOW? What do you see at this exact moment? What are you doing as we speak - write - in this journal together? In short sentences, describe your situation.

Now that we got the basics down, how can you turn your NOW into an adventurous magick-land?

Could your house be a castle that is yours? Will your car change into a pirate-ship you occupy? Is the weather fairy giving you a winter-wonder land that you get to *ooh* and *ahh* over? Or the hall closet now possesses great magnetism and unusual powers?

Remember, you can make *ALL* of life into *ALL* that you want it to be!

_____
_____
_____
_____
_____
_____
_____
_____
_____
_____
_____
_____
_____
_____

Magick and Broomsticks - The Portal to Your Wild Side

 ay 17

WHAT LITTLE AND big signs are capturing your awareness and how can you make sure to squeeze the most adventure out of those moments? Could they be:

- A sparkling rock, blinding you to see the light more vividly
- A penny that's a million dollars in disguise
- A feather, proof that you were a flying phoenix in past times
- A rice kernel that's actually worth gold
- A drop of spit from your pet, disguised as a blessing from the ocean gods

You get the point—be dramatic, go extreme, and make these split seconds count as the biggest adventure they can be.

Trust me, life's amazing like that!

_____
_____
_____
_____
_____
_____
_____
_____
_____
_____
_____

Magick and Broomsticks - The Portal to Your Wild Side

 ay 18

MAKE your littlest and most normal things in life a magick adventure! From a bathroom trip that's turning into a hike for survival, to drinking your coffee or tea like it's a marvelous magickal elixir—you can always change your physical reality into being something of the funnest nature.

Come on, you can do this! It's possible to live an extraordinary life no matter the circumstances.

___

Magick and Broomsticks - The Portal to Your Wild Side

Day 19

Do you ever feel like you are helping everyone, or that the whole world asks for your support on a constant level, and that you - as your wholesomeness - are endlessly claimed by everyone always needing you?

Now that I have your attention we can get real candid here!

This *being needed* life is actually your hero trip through the galaxies, one that shows how legendary your presence is and the fabled life you are meant to life.

Embrace that!

Magick and Broomsticks - The Portal to Your Wild Side

# Day 20

IT'S ALWAYS BEING SAID and out there for you:

Make the little things count!

But what about your big wishes and dreams? What are they and what magick will they give you once manifested? Even better, what enchantments are for you on the way there—and for the sake of fairytales, what glitter can YOU produce in your fabulous storybook called life?

Magick and Broomsticks - The Portal to Your Wild Side

Day 21

ALL THE LITTLE and big annoying scenes - like someone being rude, can't find what you are looking for, or job and family changes - are chimeric incidents that formed from parts of various different physical life realities.

Wow, there is so much wowness in that explanation that it's almost expected to want to have more of them, since they are such a glorious part of a magickal life—and hey, you might even take your speedster of a broomstick and start to chase after them.

Yes, I am giggling as I write this but seriously, how can and will you make these annoying times fascinating too?

_____
_____
_____
_____
_____
_____
_____
_____
_____
_____
_____
_____
_____
_____
_____
_____

Magick and Broomsticks - The Portal to Your Wild Side

Day 22

Have you ever realized that someone who cuts you off is on a more desperate mythical ride than you—like their hero ride at that given moment is in need of more speed, importance, or gladiator energy?

Next time this happens wish them speed, and in thought accompany them on your broomstick to keep the roads free so they can go even faster and more heroically; worth a try since you shift to supernatural when spreading and sharing such a helpful energy with your surroundings.

Magick and Broomsticks - The Portal to Your Wild Side

 ay 23

You are energy and ONE with all, just as everything and everyone is too. You are also limitless as that essence and can share and spread like butter—but more limitless since butter comes in tiny containers, or at most in buckets, which is still limited. Yes, I love butter, you just caught me!

That capability of being everywhere and nowhere at the same time is your otherworldly talent, and definitely feels like the captivating flair that you are.

How will and can you show up in your full magick-suit of infinity today, and every day after?

_____
_____
_____
_____
_____
_____
_____
_____
_____
_____
_____
_____
_____
_____
_____
_____
_____

Magick and Broomsticks - The Portal to Your Wild Side

 ay 24

FOOD IS MAGICK! That means you are a magick-enjoyer by heart since you eat, and eat, and eat all your life. Sure, there is food that's healthier, but ultimately it's a personal preference since it depends on what nourishment makes you happy, what kind of daily bread shifts you to feeling well, and what food-cleanliness you are in need of.

What fits your magick-belly best?

___

Magick and Broomsticks - The Portal to Your Wild Side

 Day 25

CLIMBING up the stairs or ascending in an elevator is the equivalent of you flying into the sky—just think about it!

Racing down the escalator or descending in a lift means you are dropping deeper into Mother Earth's nourishing essence.

Wow! I am pretty inspired about this, are you?

Magick and Broomsticks - The Portal to Your Wild Side

Day 26

WHEN YOU HEAR a loud *vroom* of a motorcycle, car, or any other engine, it is your clue to fire up your broomstick and speed into more magick! Yes, this is so, even in the middle of the night. I say take that invitation and start your flying broom!

Where are you off to?

__Magick and Broomsticks - The Portal to Your Wild Side__

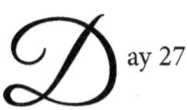

Day 27

NATURE SHOWS off magick in its best form—and you are invited to catch onto it. Listen to the enchanting bird singing and sing with it; watch the playfulness out there, and start playing too; taste the sweetness and become sweet the same way; sense the ocean, become wide and flow as well. There are numerous magick-idols out there in nature—what are those idols for you?

___

__Magick and Broomsticks - The Portal to Your Wild Side__

 ay 28

ARE YOU WAITING FOR MAGICK?

"When *this* or *that* happens I will feel amazing."

Those words or thoughts are your queue that you are indeed waiting.

How will you stop your stagnancy and, instead, get magicking?

Magick and Broomsticks - The Portal to Your Wild Side

 Day 29

Are you taking a pass on the magick that could be?

"Oh well," "It's a drag," and "It is what it is," are some of the sayings indicating that you are missing out on possible magick—because every situation in life can be shifted into a charming experience on your hero journey in which you catch magick while flying into the sunset on your glorious broomstick.

Will you try to go for it more often?

Magick and Broomsticks - The Portal to Your Wild Side

Day 30

WHEN THE SUN gives you its bright attention, it's like you are being blessed with THE worthy spotlight a star like you deserves—and since the sun shines all the time, you really have no excuses to not feel like a star.

Grab your broomstick, stand in your magick, and BE you!

_____
_____
_____
_____
_____
_____
_____
_____
_____
_____
_____
_____
_____
_____
_____
_____
_____
_____

Magick and Broomsticks - The Portal to Your Wild Side

* * *

Ready to continue on your self-growth path? Get the next journal in this series: ***The Silver Lining - And How to Find it***

BONUS

Because hey, no one ever wants the goodness to end.

Magick!
You can make it never-ending, *so keep turning the page!*

ay 31

BEING MAGICKAL, otherworldly, wizard-like, creator-strong, silly, goofy, radiant, magnetized, vitalized, enchantedly full of yourself, and in complete love with your charming you - as well as thinking the most heroically of yourself - is magickal, because that is claiming your birthright!

What are you waiting for—you ready, magick-maker?

Magick and Broomsticks - The Portal to Your Wild Side

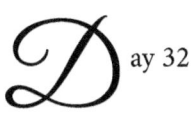 ay 32

TAKE your magickal time to practice becoming a world renowned wizard! But *heads-up*, I did not say "miss any spellbinding seconds."

Your NOW is the only magick that's always available. So go for it, super-enchanter! You so got this.

_____
_____
_____
_____
_____
_____
_____
_____
_____
_____
_____
_____
_____
_____
_____
_____
_____
_____
_____
_____

Magick and Broomsticks - The Portal to Your Wild Side

 Day 33

How many times will you grab your broomstick to fly high and infuse your personality, words, actions, and thoughts with your magick today?

Your broomstick says "Let's go—I'm supercharged!"

Your magick says, "I'm always ready whenever you are!"

So what's taking you so long? Go, go, go!

Magick and Broomsticks - The Portal to Your Wild Side

# Day 34

BECOMING ONE with your magick means that you become ONE with everything—since your magick IS your inner you and also your bridge-portal to consciousness, which holds all wisdom of everything there is: the physical and energetical.

Try it! Close your eyes and lay your body flat. Breathe yourself into your magick. Once there, sense how you are ONE with everything. Embrace that deep relaxation and realize that right then and there you are filled to the brim with the enchantment of consciousness. It's an essence where limitless magick is on every split-second menu.

Are you feeling it yet?

_____
_____
_____
_____
_____
_____
_____
_____
_____
_____
_____
_____
_____
_____
_____
_____

Magick and Broomsticks - The Portal to Your Wild Side

Day 35

NAY-SAYERS, negative-ers, and down-ers also possess magick—they are just living it in a different way. Does that mean you have to be less charming around them? No! It just means you have to brush off their sometimes-different magickal reaction, since it comes from a contrasting magickal space. So with an *I-dont-care* and an *I-let-them-be*, turn your head towards your own magick to focus on your magick-ship with yourself—in which you love yourself enough to create even more spellbinding you-ness to enjoy.

Oh, what a glorious wizard you are!

Magick and Broomsticks - The Portal to Your Wild Side

AND NOW IT'S YOUR TURN!

The following are your magickal pages to jet off even higher.

 ay 36

MAGICK IS...

Magick and Broomsticks - The Portal to Your Wild Side

 Day 37

MAGICK CREATES...

Magick and Broomsticks - The Portal to Your Wild Side

 ay 38

Magick does...

Magick and Broomsticks - The Portal to Your Wild Side

 Day 39

Magick starts...

Magick and Broomsticks - The Portal to Your Wild Side

 ay 40

MAGICK HEALS...

___

Magick and Broomsticks - The Portal to Your Wild Side

* * *

Don't forget to leave a review on Amazon.com and Goodreads.com as soon as you can, as your kind feedback helps other readers find my books easier. Thank you!

ALSO BY JACQUELINE PIRTLE

365 Days of Happiness
Because happiness is a piece of cake!

This passage book invites you to create a daily habit to live your every day joy, and is the parent companion to *365 Days of Happiness*, the journal workbook.

* * *

365 Days of Happiness - Special Edition
Because happiness is a piece of cake

This beautiful Special Edition of the bestseller *365 Days of Happiness: Because happiness is a piece of cake* has room for your notes after every daily passage.

* * *

365 Days of Happiness - Journal Workbook
Because happiness is a piece of cake

This enlightening journal workbook is your daily tool to create a habit of living your every day bliss, and is the companion to *365 Days of Happiness: Because happiness is a piece of cake*.

* * *

Life IS Beautiful - Here's to New Beginnings

If you like digging deeper into the meaning of life and are inspired by spirituality, then you'll love Jacqueline's effective teachings.

* * *

Parenting Through the Eyes of Lollipops

A Guide to Conscious Parenting

If you like harmony at home and laughter in the house, then you'll love Jacqueline's inspirational methods.

* * *

What it Means to BE a Woman

And Yes! Women do Poop!

If you like to live free, empowered, and want to decide for yourself, then you'll love Jacqueline's liberating ways.

* * *

Life-changing Journals

What. If. - Turning your IFs into it IS!
Open - Where it all starts!
To BE and Live - The reason you are here!
High for Life - The best case scenario!
Bragging - Because you're worth it!
Of Course - Because why wait...
Align, Expand, and Calibrate - Your Stairway to Joy
The Silver Lining - And How to Find it

Every journal comes in two lengths:

A 30 day journal

A 90 day journal - The Extended Edition

If you like being in charge of your own life, turning your dreams into reality, enjoy journaling, and want to squeeze the most out of your time, then you'll love Jacqueline's uplifting teachings.

ABOUT THE AUTHOR

Bestselling author, podcaster, and holistic practitioner, Jacqueline Pirtle, has twenty-four years of experience helping thousands of clients discover their own happiness. Jacqueline is the owner of **FreakyHealer** and has shared her solid teachings through her podcast *The Daily Freak*, sessions, workshops, presentations, and books with clients all over the world. She holds international degrees in holistic health and natural living. Her effective healing work has been featured in print and online magazines, podcasts, radio shows, on TV, and in the documentary *The Overly Emotional Child by Learning Success*, available on Amazon Prime.

For any questions you might have, to sign up for Jacqueline's newsletter, and for more information on whatever else she is up to, visit www.freakyhealer.com and her social media accounts @freakyhealer.

www.ingramcontent.com/pod-product-compliance
Lightning Source LLC
Chambersburg PA
CBHW071423070526
44578CB00003B/672